DENISE ALL

ROMAN GLASS IN BRITAIN

SHIRE ARCHAEOLOGY

Cover photograph
A glass jug found near Kingsbury Manor, St Albans, in a stone coffin containing
a third-century AD burial.
(Copyright St Albans Museum Service)

British Library Cataloguing in Publication Data:
Allen, Denise
Roman glass in Britain. – (Shire archaeology; no. 76)
1. Glassware, Greco-Roman – Great Britain
2. Classical antiquities
3. Great Britain – Antiquities, Roman
I. Title 748.2'9'9361
ISBN 0 7478 0373 0

Published by
SHIRE PUBLICATIONS LTD
Cromwell House, Church Street, Princes Risborough,
Buckinghamshire HP27 9AA, UK.
Website: www.shirebooks.co.uk
Email: shire@shirebooks.co.uk

Series Editor: James Dyer.

ISBN 0 7478 0373 0

First published 1998.

Printed in Great Britain by
CIT Printing Services Ltd, Press Buildings,
Merlins Bridge, Haverfordwest, Pembrokeshire SA61 1XF.

Contents

List of illustrations

Acknowledgements

This book has drawn extensively on the published and unpublished work of other scholars, as well as my own unpublished PhD thesis. Special acknowledgement must go to Donald Harden and Dorothy Charlesworth, who pioneered the study of Roman glass in Britain, and to John Shepherd, Hilary Cool and Jennifer Price. Drs Cool and Price have published large quantities of excavated glass as part of the Romano-British Glass Project, pushing glass studies fast forward in the process, whilst John Shepherd, with his colleague Gilbert Burroughes, has been involved in the experimental archaeology of Roman glass production methods. Much of their work is included in this book.

In addition, Jennifer Price kindly read the text for me. Any errors which remain are my own.

The line drawings are all by the author, whilst thanks are due to David Allen, the Castle Museum, Colchester, Verulamium Museum, Winchester City Museum, the British Museum and the National Museum of Wales for the photographs.

Thanks also to my family for their patience, and for letting me have occasional access to the word processor.

1
Origins and history

The properties of glass, neither true solid nor true liquid, make it one of the most versatile materials manufactured by humankind. It has been described as a fourth state of matter, in addition to solids, liquids and gases: a super-cooled liquid, completely fluid at high temperatures, flowing less and less as it cools, until it becomes strong enough to hold its shape for centuries. It can thus be moulded, pinched or stretched into any shape whilst hot, and engraved, cut or painted when cold. Non-absorbent, and therefore waterproof, it does not taint its contents with any unwanted taste. Its only weakness lies in the ease with which it shatters when exposed to sudden stress.

The earliest glass
In ancient times the manufacture of glass was a relatively simple process, involving the fusion of two main ingredients – fine sand, or silica, and soda, either from natural desert deposits of natron, or from soda-rich plants, such as salicornia. Lime was also needed, as a hardener, and to prevent the glass dissolving in water. This was obtained from limestone, or possibly occasionally sea-shells. Pliny the Elder, the Roman scientist and writer, gives us a very neat, though impractical, explanation in his *Historia Naturalis* as to how this magical combination was first brought about. He describes a beach at the mouth of the river Belus, south of Ptolemais (modern Acre) on the Phoenician coast, where the sand was scoured clean by the sea.

Once a ship belonging to some traders in natural soda put in here, and they scattered along the shore to prepare a meal. There were no stones to support their cooking pots, so they placed lumps of soda from their ship under them. When these became hot and fused with the sand on the beach, streams of an unknown transparent liquid flowed, and this was the origin of glass.

Writing during the first century AD, Pliny was describing a discovery that had been made perhaps three thousand years earlier, under circumstances which are now lost to us. Only a few products of this very early glass industry now survive, along with tiny fragments of texts describing the manufacturing processes.

It is generally accepted that the discovery of glass as an independent substance was the outcome of the use of glaze on pottery. The earliest written information on glassmaking techniques comes from a

Mesopotamian tablet of the seventeenth century BC giving a recipe for glaze, found near Tell'Umar on the river Tigris.

Glass was first produced to imitate precious and semi-precious stones – a function it still sometimes performs today. It was made into beads and into pieces of inlay to decorate objects of metal and wood. The 'cradle of civilisation' in western Asia (now Iraq and Syria) was the most likely birthplace of the glass industry, between 3000 and 2500 BC.

The first glass vessels appeared there during the late sixteenth century BC and, following the conquest of the area by Pharaoh Tuthmosis III, were soon copied in Egypt. Glass workshops flourished intermittently in both those areas down to the mid first century BC and in addition spread, from the seventh century BC, into the eastern and central Mediterranean.

Early techniques

Early glass vessels were manufactured using three main techniques, all of them laborious and slow, ensuring that the products were rare and costly:

Core- and rod-formed vessels were made by building up molten glass, by either dipping or trailing, around a core of mud and straw fixed on a metal rod. Bright colours, with zigzagging contrasting trails, were popular. The core was removed after the glass had cooled, and handles, rims and bases were added. Most of the vessels made in this way were small unguent and scent containers (figure 1.1-3).

Cold-cut vessels were produced from raw blocks of glass, or from thick moulded blanks, using techniques borrowed from stone- and gem-cutters. A variety of small containers could be made in this way (figure 1.4).

Cast glass vessels and objects were probably made in a variety of ways, and several possible production methods have been suggested by glass historians. The most likely for open vessel shapes, such as bowls and plates, involved the primary manufacture of a circular blank of glass. This could either be monochrome or a mosaic made of sections cut from fused bundles of thin glass rods, arranged in elaborate coloured patterns, then heated and fused together. The disc blanks, either plain or polychrome, would then be sagged over, into or through a former or mould, in a furnace, thus taking the required vessel shape. After cooling, the surfaces would be ground and polished to a smooth finish (figure 1.5).

Hellenistic glass

The Hellenistic glass industry of the late fourth to mid first centuries BC flourished in the central and eastern Mediterranean area, particularly on the Syrian coast and at Alexandria, on the Egyptian coast. Its products

1. Early glass vessels, scale ½. 1 Core-formed kohl-flask, Egypt, 1350-1225 BC. 2 Core-formed alabastron, eastern Mediterranean, sixth to fifth century BC. 3 Core-formed oinochoe, eastern Mediterranean, fourth to third century BC. 4 Alabastron, cold-cut from a solid blank of glass, Syria or Assyria, seventh to sixth century BC. 5 Mosaic bowl, Assur, Iraq, seventh century BC.

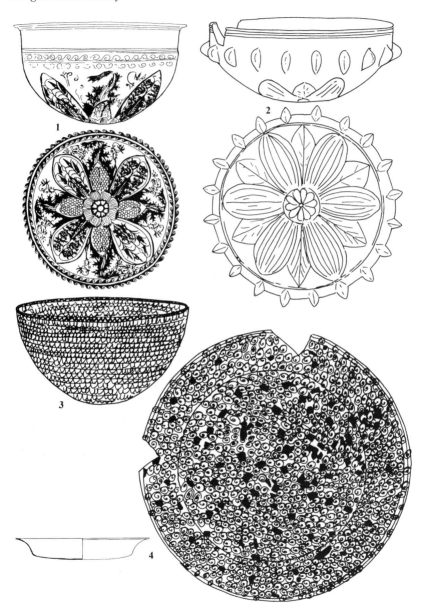

2. Hellenistic glass vessels, from a burial group found at Canosa, southern Italy, later third century BC. Scale ¼. 1 Sandwich gold glass bowl. 2 Segmental bowl with band of bosses. 3 Hemispherical laced mosaic bowl. 4 Shallow mosaic dish (profile scale ⅛).

were the immediate antecedents of the Roman industry and included some core-formed unguent bottles, but most common were hemispherical bowls, occasionally with gold-leaf decoration sandwiched between two layers of glass, plates with outsplayed sides, and cups with carved wing handles. One of the most important groups of vessels of this date comprises ten bowls, dishes and cups found in a tomb of the third century BC at Canosa, southern Italy, purchased by the British Museum in 1871 and presently on display there (figure 2).

The earliest glass in Britain

The only glass to reach Britain at this early, pre-Roman date came in the form of beads and, rarely, bangles. Some beads were imported from as early as the second millennium BC and are found in bronze age contexts. Throughout the iron age period, from 700 BC to the Roman invasions, highly decorated beads were both imported from the continent and manufactured on British sites (figure 3). Vivid evidence for the latter was found during excavations at Hengistbury Head, near Christchurch, Dorset, an important trading and production centre for many commodities. Lumps of raw, unworked glass, likely to have been parts of larger cast ingots, were identified amongst the continental imports in late iron age contexts. Some may have been used to make artefacts on the site, whilst others were intended to be traded and worked elsewhere.

The invention of glass-blowing

Around the middle of the first century BC a discovery was made that revolutionised the glass-vessel industry: molten glass could be inflated into an almost infinite variety of shapes, each complete vessel taking a fraction of the time needed for previous production methods. At a stroke glass vessels became cheap, practical, attractive alternatives to those of pottery and metal. Exactly how the discovery of glass-blowing came

3. Iron age glass beads found in Britain, fourth to third century BC. Scale ¹/₂.

about is not known for certain, but it seems likely that it first involved the inflation of the ends of long thin glass tubes. Excavations in 1971 in the Jewish Quarter of the Old City of Jerusalem produced a heap of glass-working debris showing clear evidence of tube-blowing, dating to the first half of the first century BC. The use of separate iron blowpipes was a later development. The evidence of surviving vessels indicates that glass-blowing began in one of the Syrian workshops, marking the beginning of a period of intense experimentation and innovation, followed by the rapid spread of workshops throughout the Mediterranean region.

The spread of the Roman glass industry

The glass-blowing revolution coincided perfectly with a time of rapid change in Rome. The Republic was drawing its last few breaths, Julius Caesar was campaigning in north-western Europe, and Pompey the Great was annexing eastern provinces. The free exchange of influences and materials throughout the known world which characterised the Roman Empire was fast becoming established. Glass-workers quickly recognised the potential markets first in Italy, and then the rest of Europe, and moved accordingly. By the end of the first century BC, at some time during the reign of Augustus, glass workshops had been set up in Rome itself, in Campania in southern Italy and in the Po Valley region of northern Italy. They were producing blown glass vessels alongside those made by older, casting methods. In the early to mid first century AD the first glasshouses north of the Alps were established in what is now Switzerland, and then at sites in northern Europe, in Germany, France and Belgium. Local availability of the raw materials for glassmaking was not an important criterion, as long as there was a route by which the ingredients could be shipped in and the finished articles traded out. Thus Cologne, on the river Rhine in Germany, became one of the most prolific manufacturing centres of the Roman period. Much of the glass found in Roman Britain was imported from the Continent, but more and more evidence is emerging for the local manufacture of some vessels.

2

Manufacture and trade

The pattern of manufacturing centres and trade routes for glass has proved more difficult to establish than for many other contemporary Roman industries. To understand why, it is first necessary to examine the production process in more detail.

Glass-vessel manufacture

There are very few surviving ancient illustrations of Roman glass furnaces. One, a small terracotta from Egypt, of the first or second century AD, is interpreted as showing Eros holding a blowing iron and crucible beside a glass furnace (figure 4). Another, from a late first-century pottery lamp found at Asseria, Dalmatia, shows a small two-tiered furnace with a seated figure apparently blowing glass (figure 5). No technical details are visible in either, and it is therefore tempting to turn to later manuscripts for these. Some procedures are likely to have remained virtually unchanged until the industrial revolution, but others are harder to support from the archaeological record.

Probably the most famous illustration of pre-industrial glassmaking comes from one of a series of miniatures showing the travels of Sir John Mandeville in the fifteenth century. He visited a glassworks in Bohemia (the modern Czech Republic), where the glassmaking process is clearly shown (figure 6). At this time three distinct stages were involved:

Fritting. The raw ingredients were first fused together at a temperature of about 600°C, then broken into lumps to be used at the melting furnace or stored for future use. It is still uncertain whether this stage was necessary for Roman soda-lime glass, and no evidence for it has yet been found.

4. (Above) Terracotta from Egypt, first to second century AD, showing Eros holding a blowpipe and crucible, beside a glass furnace with two openings. Scale ¼.

5. (Right) Pottery lamp from Asseria, Dalmatia, first century AD, showing a glass-blower beside a furnace. Scale ½.

6. Miniature from Bohemia, fifteenth century, showing a glassworks and all the stages of glass-vessel manufacture. (Copyright British Library 24189 f16)

Melting and blowing. The fritted glass was put into crucibles, to be heated to a temperature high enough to achieve fluidity – about 1100-1300°C. Broken glass, or cullet, was added to speed up the melting process, since glass melts at a lower temperature than its separate constituents. This procedure was certainly followed in Roman times too and has many consequences for the study of glass-working. Waste material from the manufacturing process was reused rather than left lying around in large quantities, making the recognition of production sites more difficult. Even when collections of broken fragments have been found at possible glass-manufacturing centres, they cannot be identified with certainty as the products of that workshop. The Roman writers Statius and Martial both describe a system akin to modern bottle banks, whereby broken glass vessels were collected and exchanged for barter. This practice also helps to explain the dearth of relatively complete glass vessels on Roman domestic sites. The fragments which are found are the 'ones that got away', and restorable broken vessels are rare. In addition, attempts to identify the sources of glass vessels by chemical analysis are thwarted, as glass originally made at sites all over the Empire could end up in the same molten batch.

The Mandeville manuscript shows simple pottery crucibles within the main furnace. The evidence for Roman times indicates that sometimes crucibles were made for the purpose, out of ceramics which could withstand high temperatures, sometimes selected domestic pots were used, and some Roman furnaces contained rectangular tanks for the molten glass.

The colour of the glass would also be controlled at this melting stage, in ancient as well as post-medieval times. The presence of impurities of iron in sand results in batches of blue-green colour, and many Roman vessels, particularly the more utilitarian containers, are found in variations of this shade. Glassmakers from very early times had learnt to counteract this by adding metallic oxides such as cobalt, copper and antimony, resulting in a variety of strong bright colours, or alternatively a clear, colourless glass.

The furnace illustrated in the Mandeville manuscript is very simple, with a stoke-hole to the lower right, and two openings with pots of molten glass, which the glass-blowers are gathering on to their blowpipes. After inflation the vessel body would be removed from the blowpipe, often with the aid of a solid metal pontil rod attached to the underside via a wad of hot glass. Handles and other details would be added, and the finished article would be ready for the last part of the process.

Annealing. Glass vessels must be left to cool gradually, otherwise strains set up within the glass would cause them to crack and break. In medieval and post-medieval times a cooler annealing oven was therefore provided, sometimes to one side of the furnace, as shown in the illustration, or sometimes above it, in a third storey. Similar provision must have been made in Roman times, but very little evidence has survived. One possibility has been suggested by excavations at a site in Israel, destroyed by an earthquake during the seventh century AD. Finished glass vessels were found lying in a pit filled with ashes and charred olive pips, where they may have been cooling when natural disaster struck.

The glass industry in Roman Britain

From the procedures described above, the evidence for glassmaking could be expected to fall into three main categories: the remains of furnaces, perhaps with annealing ovens; tools, including crucibles, blowpipes, pontil rods, pincers and shears; and ingredients, including both raw materials (sand, soda and lime), lumps of glass frit or ingots of glass, and collections of cullet, in the form of either the side-products of manufacture or broken vessel fragments. Unfortunately no site of Roman date in Britain has ever been found with all these items in association. The scattered evidence is summarised in figure 7.

The furnaces need not be very large, as they were required to heat only pots or small tanks of glass, not to fire the vessels themselves.

7. Glassworking sites in Britain. Key to map: 1 Caistor-by-Norwich (tank furnace); 2 Castor, Water Newton (furnace and crucible); 3 Colchester (glass-blowing waste); 4 Leicester (furnace and glass-blowing waste); 5 London (more than sixteen sites associated with glass-working, including furnaces, glass-blowing waste); 6 Mancetter (furnace, glass-blowing waste); 7 Silchester (furnace and crucible fragments); 8 Worcester (crucible fragments); 9 Wilderspool, near Warrington (possible glass furnaces); 10 Wroxeter (sand for glassmaking, glass-blowing waste); 11 York (crucible fragments); 12 Bulmore, Caerleon (glass-blowing waste).

They were made of clay and were usually oval or keyhole-shaped. British examples include more than half a dozen from various sites in London (figure 8) and one each from Mancetter (Warwickshire), Leicester, Castor (Water Newton, Cambridgeshire) and Caistor-by-Norwich. Several of these were in close association with other industries, particularly pottery kilns. Some had crucibles and/or glass waste with them, but these also occur as isolated finds.

No metal tools have been found at British sites, and indeed blowing irons have been found at very few Roman sites, such as Merida in Spain and Salona in former Yugoslavia. Some wooden tools were probably used, and these would not be expected to survive under normal circumstances.

The only possible find of one of the raw materials for glassmaking in Britain is a small pile of white sand from Wroxeter in Shropshire, and it seems that any use of this for glassmaking was experimental, and not very successful. Similar experimentation with raw materials may have been recognised at the Coppergate site in York, dating to the late second

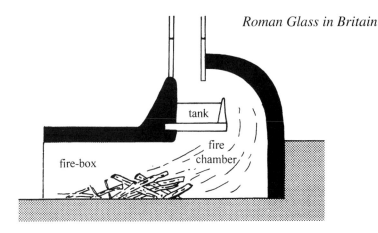

8. Sketch section through a reconstructed glass furnace – a small keyhole-shaped structure, about 1.5 metres long, with a suspended tank for molten glass. Based on the evidence from second-century AD sites in London. (After John Shepherd and Gilbert Burroughes)

or early third century. However, the lack of evidence for the manufacture of glass from basic materials, together with the relative profusion of collections of broken fragments and glass-blowing waste, suggests that the industry in Britain consisted of glass-working using recycled glass fragments.

Collections of cullet, usually stored in a pit, have been recognised at a number of sites. They comprise ordinary broken vessel fragments, together with pieces of waste glass from the blowing process. The latter are called moiles, and the commonest shape is a small cylinder that was

9. Moiles and droplets: examples of glass waste found in a pit at Sheepen, Colchester, Essex, second century AD. Scale $1/2$.

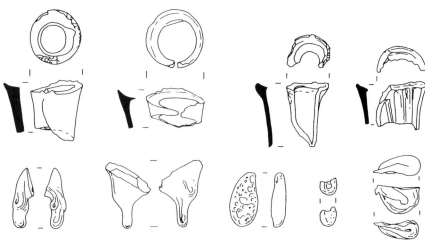

left attached to the blowpipe after the vessel body, or paraison, had been removed. Drips of glass and distorted body fragments are also found. Samples from an assemblage found in a pit at Sheepen, Colchester, Essex, in a field with pottery kilns, are illustrated in figure 9. The largest single assemblage of such material from Britain was found in 1993 at Guildhall Yard, London, just outside the Roman amphitheatre, and comprised 50 kg of glass fragments. This included broken vessel fragments, workshop and furnace waste and glass left in crucibles, all of which had been smashed with a hammer before burial. Both this and the Sheepen assemblage belong to the second century AD.

The overall picture for the manufacture of glass in Roman Britain, therefore, suggests the production of a range of simple blown vessels, as well as window glass, using recycled fragments, presumably for local consumption. This appears to have been established from the beginning of the second century AD, and the number of sites at which this has been recognised is increasing as the scant evidence is identified by more excavators and glass specialists.

Trade in glass

The majority of vessels, including the finer wares with elaborate decorations, must have been imported into Britain from elsewhere in the Roman world. Again, the physical remains of glassmaking sites are rare, and only the distribution patterns of some categories of glass vessel provide clues to their probable place of origin.

Glass vessels made at sites throughout the Empire could reach Britain in a number of ways. The movement of troops and administrators, together with their households, meant that individual glasses, or groups of domestic items, could arrive in Britain from anywhere in the Mediterranean world as personal possessions. In addition many vessels arrived through organised trade, but distinction has to be drawn between those usually finer items that were imported in their own right as tableware and those, such as unguent bottles, larger bottles and flasks, which were imported for their contents. The latter represent trade in a variety of liquid and semi-liquid commodities, to which the glass containers were incidental. Many have moulded or stamped trademarks, some of which offer clues as to the manufacturers of the vessels, others to the producers of the contents.

The available evidence for the glass-vessel trade suggests that most of the brightly coloured pieces found in Britain from the first decade or so after the conquest were imported from Italy, where the industry was thriving (see chapter 3). As mentioned in chapter 1, soon after the mid first century AD workers had established themselves at centres north of the Alps and began to produce their own vessel forms, which do not appear further south. Most of the finer vessels found in Britain from this time can be matched by numerous finds from Cologne and many other sites in the Rhineland and northern France, from where they are likely to have been imported.

Attempts to identify sites of workshops for specific types of vessels could be fruitless if the possibility of itinerant glass-workers is considered. The list of finishing and decorative techniques on pages 58-9 includes some that were an integral part of the manufacture of the vessel, carried out whilst the glass was still hot and pliable. Others, such as carving, cutting, engraving and painting, could be added at any time after completion of the vessel and may sometimes have been carried out away from the glassmaking site. Several hypotheses are therefore available. Travelling glass-blowers with their own specialised styles could have set up at a number of sites to supply local markets. They would have taken their tools with them, including moulds for mould-blowing. In addition, cast or blown vessel blanks could have been carried around by specialist glass-cutters or painters and finished at a number of sites to satisfy customer demand. Occasionally relatively small groups of common vessel types were given decoration that can be identified as the work of a single artist or group of artists, and this seems certain to indicate some separate private enterprise.

The Roman period in Britain lasted nearly four centuries, and there were many changes in all aspects of the material culture during that time. This was true of fashions in glass vessels, and the discussion of what has been found in the province has therefore been divided into four convenient periods. These should by no means be taken as absolute divisions as new forms were constantly evolving, peaking in popularity and then declining. They are merely a simplified indication of some of the overall trends in what is a staggering range of glass-vessel forms and decorations.

Glass vessels began to be used regularly in Britain from very soon after the conquest, and this continued until the end of the Roman period. Survival is patchy, for reasons already discussed, and the most complete vessels from all periods are those that were included in burials. These were most often either containers reused as cinerary urns or unguent bottles. Unfortunately fine glass vessels were not given as grave-goods in Britain as frequently as on the Continent. This may reflect their relative rarity, their high value, or meanness on the part of the bereaved, but the result is that cases full of complete Roman glass vessels are an uncommon sight in British museums. However, the evidence from both civilian settlements and military sites does show that glassware of the very finest quality was circulating in Britain throughout the Roman period, albeit often represented in the archaeological record only by fragments.

3

Glass vessels AD 43–70

The first glass vessels to come into Britain may have been personal gifts and arrived some decades before the successful invasion of AD 43. The earliest find to date is a cast and ground ribbed bowl of yellow-green glass from a burial of 50-20 BC at Hertford Heath, Hertfordshire (figure 10). It was probably made before 70 BC at the eastern end of the Mediterranean and had travelled far as a treasured possession before it was buried in southern England. Fragments of two small coloured unguent bottles were recorded from early first-century AD burials at Mount Bures, near Colchester, Essex, and at Hurstbourne Tarrant, Hampshire, but both are now lost. A very few fragments have come from pre-conquest levels at settlement sites in southern England, but the impression left by the archaeological record suggests that glass vessels were very rare in Britain before AD 43.

The most important assemblage of early glass vessel fragments from

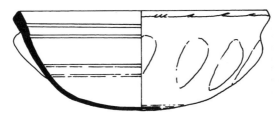

10. Glass bowl from an iron age burial of 50-20 BC at Hertford Heath, Hertfordshire, the earliest glass vessel found in Britain to date. Scale $^1/_2$.

Britain was excavated at Sheepen, Colchester, Essex, during the 1930s and in 1970, from the site of the late iron age oppidum and early Roman settlement known as Camulodunum. With the exception of two fragments from pre-conquest levels, the glass came from contexts dated between the invasion of AD 43 and soon after the Boudican uprising of AD 60/61. Examples of most of the forms and decorative groups discussed in this chapter were found there. The Roman town of Colchester itself and many other sites in southern England have yielded further examples. In Wales, northern England and Scotland, where the Roman presence took longer to become established, there have been fewer finds of mid first-century types, but enough to prove that some survived for a long period after their date of manufacture.

During the first few decades after the conquest the glass industry was

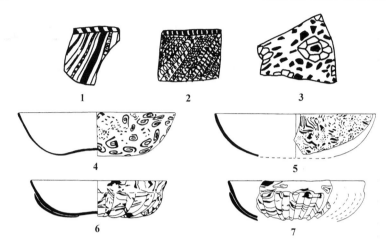

11. Cast polychrome glass. 1-3 Fragments of strip-, lace- and floral-mosaic glass, scale ^{1}/$_2$. 4-7 Bowls and fragments of spiral-mosaic, dappled and marbled glass, scale ^{1}/$_4$.

enjoying a phase of vigorous experimentation. The art of blowing was still a relatively new discovery and was being employed alongside long-established casting methods. In addition it had been realised that the plasticity of molten glass was ideally suited to mould-blowing, and a variety of vessels was being produced in this way. There was a tendency to regard glass as a cheap way of imitating other materials, and many vessels were produced that were clearly copies of prototypes in pottery, metal and semi-precious stones. Much of the decoration consisted of patterns of colour within the glass, and a wide range of strong colours was employed: translucent deep blue, emerald green, dark brown, sometimes so dark that it appears 'black', purple, amber and peacock, and opaque red, yellow, white and sky blue. Natural blue-green glass was also widely used, for tablewares as well as containers.

Cast glass

The casting methods described on page 7 continued to be popular for producing open forms such as bowls, dishes and plates. Many had an elaborate polychrome decoration, resulting from the various composite patterns of rod-sections and strips of glass that had been fused together into a circular blank before the vessels themselves were formed. Six categories of cast polychrome decoration have been defined: strip mosaic, lace mosaic, floral mosaic, spiral mosaic, marbled and dappled glass (figure 11).

Strip- and lace-mosaic patterns (figure 11.1-2) were produced by

12. Blue and white marbled pillar-moulded bowl from a Flavian burial at Radnage, Buckinghamshire. (Copyright British Museum)

fusing strips of glass together; in the latter case, the strips were first twisted with a contrasting thread. This was a popular Hellenistic technique, employed to make simple shallow and deep curved bowls, and had gone out of fashion by the middle of the first century AD. These vessels were probably no longer being made by the time the Romans invaded Britain, and the few fragments found at Sheepen and other southern English sites must represent heirlooms.

Floral and spiral mosaic patterns (figure 11.3-4) were formed by fusing the cross-sections cut from composite glass rods. These could either be given a floral arrangement, with 'petals' around a contrasting centre, or a spiral section could be achieved by rolling a flat hot band of glass around a cane. Floral-mosaic bowls also originated during the Hellenistic period, but these, and spiral-mosaic patterns, were used for a wider variety of bowl, dish and plate forms.

Marbled and dappled patterns resulted from a distortion of the original mosaic design during manufacture of the vessels (figure 11.5-7). They most often occur on pillar-moulded bowls (see below). The production of polychrome cast vessels declined quite rapidly after the middle of the first century AD, but many remained in use for some considerable time, and finds occasionally occur on sites not occupied until the later first century. Figure 12 shows a fine blue and white marbled pillar-moulded bowl from a grave of the later first century found at Radnage, Buckinghamshire. Some white spirals are clearly visible within the marbling.

The pillar-moulded bowl is one of the commonest glass finds on first-century sites (figure 13.5-6). It is now thought that its manufacture began, as with other cast forms, with a disc blank, either monochrome or polychrome. This was then heated and pressed with a slotted tool, so that the ribs were extruded through the slots, causing distortion of any mosaic pattern. The ribbed disc was sagged over a convex former in the furnace, and finally, after cooling, the inside surface and both sides of the rims were rotary-polished. Often bands of horizontal lines were cut inside. The distinctive finish means that even very small fragments can easily be recognised. A great deal of variety occurs within the form: some were polychrome, some strong single colours, such as deep blue, dark brown and amber, and many were blue-green. The shape ranged from very deep to very shallow, with every variation in between. They must have been useful, sturdy, all-purpose serving vessels, but their popularity waned during the second half of the first century AD. Coloured bowls were made until about AD 60, the blue-green variety until about AD 80, and a number continued to be used until the early second century.

Other cast glass vessels were produced in shapes almost identical to those used for samian pottery, and it is likely that both groups had been influenced by metal and stone prototypes (figure 13.1, 3-4). The sharp outlines were achieved by casting blanks between two or more interlocking moulds and then, after annealing, affixing them to lathes, where they were cut and polished to their final shapes. Occasionally polychrome glass was used, but strong single colours, such as emerald green and peacock blue, were particularly popular. Opaque red or orange with red streaks was sometimes used, which emphasised the close relationship with pottery types. These vessels were popular during the middle years of the first century, but few were made after about AD 70. Those forms that did continue began to appear from this time in colourless as well as coloured glass, as discussed in chapter 4.

Mould-blown glass
A wide variety of mould-blown glasses was made during the first century AD, and, although the technique continued to be used sporadically throughout the Roman period, this was its floruit. The terracotta or metal moulds, made in two or three parts, could be used more than once, and groups of vessels made from the same mould can sometimes be identified. No manufacturing centres have been identified, and indeed the vessels could have been produced by itinerant glass-blowers (page 18), which would mean that vessels from the same mould groups could have been produced at a number of different sites.

The designs were strongly influenced by fashions in other materials, such as relief-decorated pottery and metalwork. Bowls, cups, jugs, amphorisks and unguent bottles were all made using this technique,

13. Some of the bowls and cups that were popular during the period AD 43-70: 1-6 cast; 7-8 mould-blown; 9-15 free-blown. Scale $^1/_4$.

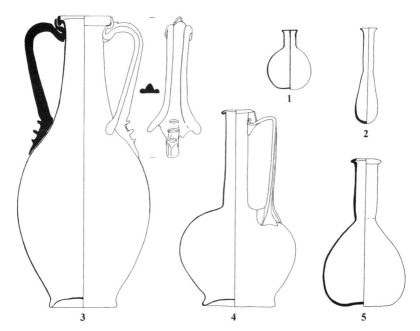

14. Some of the glass serving vessels and containers that were popular during the period AD 43-70. Scale ¹/₄.

in strong colours or blue-green glass.

Many of the early mould-blown designs incorporated inscriptions. Some of these were Greek names, especially Ennion, Jason, Meges, Aristeas and others, who could have been the mould-makers, glassblowers or workshop proprietors (figure 15). Some vessels bore mottoes in Greek, including such exhortations as 'Let the buyer remember'. Many cups and bowls of this group were made during the period AD 35-45; their distribution is widespread, and at least one cup or bowl with a Greek inscription made its way to Britain – a fragment has been found at Binchester, County Durham.

15. Mould-blown cups signed by Ennion: 1 from Italy; 2 from Sidon (?). Scale ¹/₄.

Simpler mould-blown ribbed bowls and cups were also widely used throughout most of the first century AD (figure 13.8). Fragments are quite often found on British sites, and occasionally complete examples have survived.

A slightly later mould-blown group, popular during the period AD 50-70/75, has a more limited distribution, confined to western and north-western provinces. It comprises cylindrical and ovoid cups decorated with scenes of chariot-racing, gladiatorial combat or athletic contests, together with inscriptions in Latin, usually the names of famous combatants (figures 13.7, 16, 17). About three hundred complete and fragmentary examples are now known, including many from Britain. Only one British find, from Colchester, was complete (figures 16.1, 17), but fragments representing many of the mould varieties have been found.

Blown glass

At this early period blown-glass techniques were often used to mimic the effects achieved by the casting methods already described. Strong colours were popular, as well as natural blue-green glass, and a marbled or dappled effect was often achieved by the use of marvered trails and blobs (figure 13.9, 15). Other techniques exploiting colour were used, such as casing and cameo-cutting, and occasionally fragments produced by these methods have been found in Britain.

Amongst the tablewares, small coloured ribbed bowls with marvered trails (figure 13.9) were popular until about AD 50, and a few fragments appear on early Roman sites in Britain. Other forms were given classical shapes such as the two-handled cantherus, sometimes decorated with marvered trails or applied contrasting blobs (figure 13.15). Jugs, flasks and unguent bottles were also occasionally given marvered decoration.

The most popular blown-glass drinking vessel until about AD 70 was a simple cylindrical or hemispherical form, sometimes with a pointed kick to the base, with slightly inturned ground rim, the body often decorated with horizontal wheel-cut grooves or abraded bands (figure 13.11). Such vessels are often called 'Hofheim cups' after the large number found at the German site of that name. They were most often blue-green but also occur in strong colours. A very few of these vessels were given decoration in enamelled paint, comprising foliage, animals, birds, and sometimes pygmies fighting. Certain uniform elements of style suggest that they were the work of a single artist or group of artists, but their place of origin is unknown. Several complete vessels have survived, but only a few fragments have been found in Britain (figure 18). Another form of drinking vessel in use at this time was taller, also decorated with wheel-cut lines, and with a solid domed base (figure 13.10).

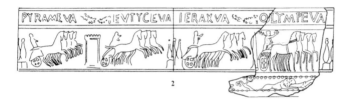

16. (Above) Friezes from mould-blown circus cups (for vessel shape see figures 13.7, 17). 1 Complete cup with two-frieze chariot race, from Colchester, Essex. 2 Fragment of cup with single-frieze chariot race, from Colchester, superimposed on to frieze of a complete vessel of the same mould group from Couvain, Belgium. 3 Fragmentary cup with pairs of gladiators fighting, from Colchester.

17. (Left) Complete cup with two-frieze chariot race, blue-green glass, from Colchester, Essex. (Copyright British Museum)

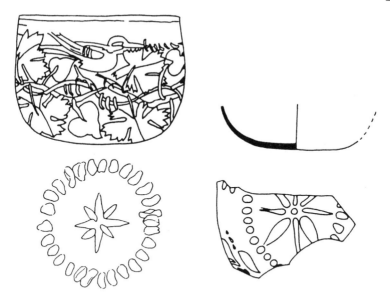

18. Cup from Locarno-Muralto, Switzerland, painted with birds and foliage, with a base fragment from a similar vessel found at Colchester, Essex. Scale ¹/₂.

Vessels that may have been used for serving drinks during this period include two-handled amphorisks, made in translucent or opaque coloured glass (figure 14.3), and thin-walled globular long-necked jugs (figure 14.4). Bowls for serving fruit and other foods include shallow and deep cylindrical vessels with folded rims, often ribbed bodies and high base-rings (figure 13.12-13). Several of these forms continued to be made into the earlier second century (page 36).

A wide variety of glass containers, usually made of blue-green glass, was introduced from the middle of the first century AD. These vessels must have been made at many centres throughout the Roman Empire and occur in their highest numbers during the period AD 70-170 (pages 31-5). However, a few were most popular during the third quarter of the first century AD, including conical-bodied flasks with folded rims (figure 14.5) and simple unguent bottles with fire-rounded rims (figure 14.1-2). The latter are often found with cremation burials of the second half of the first century, usually distorted by fire. They may have held oils that were used to anoint the body during the funeral and afterwards been placed on the pyre with the body. Antiquarians in the past gave them the name 'lachrymatories', in the belief that they had been used to collect the tears of the mourners.

4
Glass vessels AD 70–170

During the last thirty years of the first century AD there was a marked change of style in popular glassware. The bright strong colours that had been popular around the middle of the century disappeared quite rapidly from the repertoire, to be replaced by colourless and pale green tinted glass. These wares had occurred regularly during Hellenistic times, and occasionally as part of some mosaic designs in the early Roman period, but now they were used for blown glass for the first time. The change may represent a technological advance, or it may have been dictated by fashion. Pliny, writing at about this time in his *Historia Naturalis*, tells us that 'the most highly valued glass is colourless and transparent, as closely as possible resembling rock crystal'.

Possibly glass was becoming more acceptable as a material in its own right, and glass-workers were no longer attempting to imitate the products of other industries to the same extent. Along with the increasingly regular appearance of colourless and pale green vessels came decorative techniques that were exclusively suited to the medium. Cutting, engraving and carving were used to produce a range of effects, and trailing and tooling were equally popular. Coloured glass was still occasionally used, often to provide details on otherwise colourless vessels, but also sometimes for the vessels themselves, and blue-green glass continued to be used extensively for containers as well as tablewares.

During the early part of this period vessels produced by the three techniques of casting, mould-blowing and blowing were still being used side by side.

Cast glass

Cast plates, bowls and cups continued to be made until the early second century, but increasingly in colourless rather than coloured glass. Some survived until the middle of the second century, as shown by fragments found on sites not occupied until that date.

Most common were plates or bowls with a wide everted rim, with or without an overhang, and a base-ring (figure 19.1-2). These were made both in strong monochrome colours and in colourless glass. Some of the latter were given elaborate cut decoration, usually in the form of regular facets that covered the outer surface, as on a fragmentary bowl from Wroxeter (figure 19.2). Occasionally they bear vegetative designs or simple facets restricted to the rim or to the rim and base area. The edge of the rim often has an 'egg and dart' pattern, and in some cases

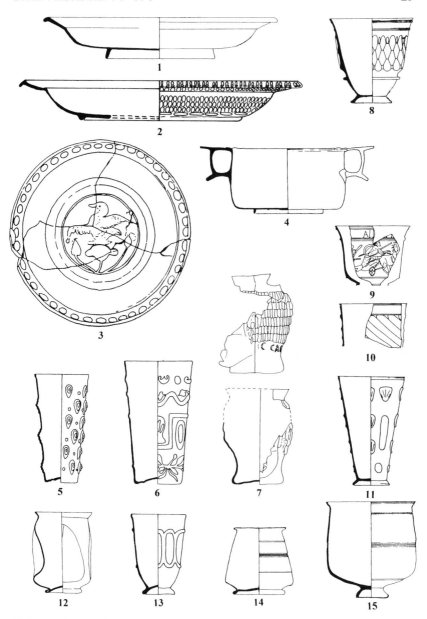

19. Some of the bowls and cups in use during the period AD 70-170: 1-4 cast; 5-7 mould-blown; 8-15 free-blown. Scale ¹/₄.

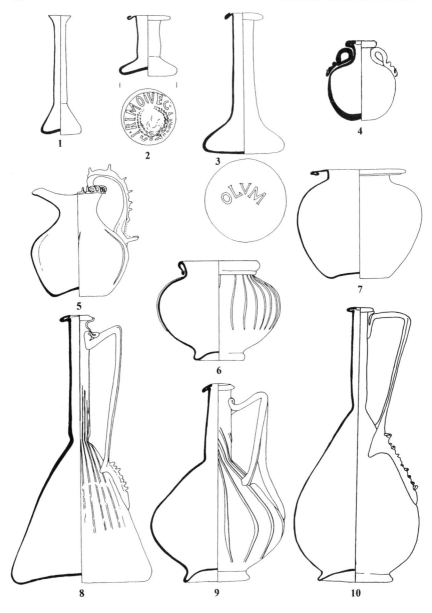

20. Some of the glass serving vessels and containers that were popular during the period AD 70-170. Scale $^1/_4$.

carved handles were incorporated. An unusual bowl from an early second-century AD grave at Girton College, Cambridge, has a base decorated with a duck with outspread wings above leaves and flowers of lotus (figure 19.3).

Other cast colourless bowls had simple splayed sides, whilst some cups had handles carved from the vessel blank. A fine complete example of a colourless scyphos came from a late first-century pit in the Middle Walbrook Valley, London (figure 19.4).

Vessels of this group are found throughout the Roman world, and their origins are not known. It has been suggested that there may have been a trade in cast blanks, which could then be finished either with or without cut decoration to meet local or individual requirements.

Mould-blown glass

Mould-blown vessels with relief decoration continued to be popular until late in the first century, but the forms differed from those described in chapter 3. Most common from about AD 65-80 were tall truncated conical beakers, often decorated with almond-shaped bosses, with or without a diamond-shaped trellis framework. Complete vessels have been found on Continental sites, and fragments occur quite regularly in Britain (figure 19.5). These vessels were made in strongly coloured and blue-green glass.

Another decorative variant used for the truncated conical beaker comprised a combination of meanders, shells, rosettes, ovals and other motifs (figure 19.6). These were quite often made in colourless glass, and the same kinds of patterns were reproduced on colourless relief-cut beakers at about the same time (figure 19.11).

Another quite rare mould-blown form of this later first-century period was the negro-head beaker. Several fragments have been found in Britain, including two inscribed with the name C Caesi Bugaddi from a rubbish pit in King William Street, London (figure 21), and from below the legionary parade ground at Caerleon, Gwent (figure 19.7).

During the second and third centuries mould-blown containers in the form of heads, bunches of grapes, fish and other novelties continued to be produced occasionally, but these are rarely found in Britain.

Mould-blown bottles

A completely separate category of mould-blown vessels comprises the bottles that make up the bulk of any Roman glass assemblage from sites occupied during the first two centuries AD. These vessels, made of blue-green glass, were blown into undecorated moulds that produced bodies of square, hexagonal, rectangular, octagonal or, very rarely, triangular section (figure 22). Separate base moulds of stone, clay or

21. Fragmentary negro-head beaker, blue-green glass, found at King William Street, London. (Copyright British Museum)

wood with negative designs cut into them were slotted into the bottom of the body moulds, to produce basal markings in relief on the bottles. These most often comprised various numbers of concentric circles, but a very wide variety of geometric designs, corner motifs, letters and sometimes inscriptions also occurs. These may have been the trademarks of the vessel makers, but it is also possible that they belonged to the proprietors of the contents. After the bodies with their bases had been formed, the shoulders and necks were produced by free manipulation, the rims finished by folding, and a ribbed angular handle, or sometimes two, added. A variety of this form was also made with a cylindrical body, free- rather than mould-blown, with a slightly concave base and no markings (figure 22.1).

These vessels were made as containers, and the wide range of shapes and sizes must reflect an equally wide range of contents, although these have never been found intact. In all vessel shapes there appears to be a division between a tall narrow variety and one that is squat. It has not proved possible to define recurring standard sizes or capacities, but this would always be difficult because so much of the evidence is fragmentary.

22. Some of the wide range of bottle shapes and sizes in circulation during the later first and second centuries, especially the period AD 70-170: 1 cylindrical, AD 40-120; 2 hexagonal, AD 70-120; 3 square, AD 40-200; 4 rectangular, AD 150-200. Scale 1/4.

23. Large hexagonal bottle reused as a cinerary urn, from Colchester, Essex. (Photograph by David Allen, reproduced with the permission of the Castle Museum, Colchester)

Many complete bottles and fragments have bands of usage scratches that bear testimony to a long period of use, and they were presumably refilled and reused a number of times. Some larger vessels were finally made use of as cinerary urns in burials of the later first and earlier second centuries (figures 23, 24). Bands of scratches around the shoulder and lower body indicate that some bottles were kept in crate-like containers and frequently withdrawn and replaced. There are occasionally marks visible around the neck beneath the rim; these must have been made by the ties securing the stoppers, perhaps made of cork or wood, sealed with pitch or resin.

The periods during which the various bottle shapes were in circulation show some variation. Cylindrical and square bottles first appeared just before the middle of the first century AD, and hexagonal bottles soon after, but they did not become common until about AD 70. From this date until the end of the first century these forms, particularly the cylinders and squares, dominated glass assemblages, often totalling between a third and a half of the surviving fragments. Cylindrical bottles then went out of use early in the second century, leaving the squares as the commonest type of glass vessel. Hexagonal bottles were never as popular as the other two, but a few examples survived to appear in mid second-century contexts, disappearing thereafter. A

24. Square bottle reused as a cinerary urn, from Colchester, Essex. (Photograph by David Allen, reproduced with the permission of the Castle Museum, Colchester)

rectangular, or occasionally octagonal, two-handled variety was made around the middle of the second century but was never common. The square bottles were probably made until some time within the second half of the second century. Fragments often appear in archaeological features of late second- or early third-century date, but it is difficult to determine whether these reflect continued use of the vessels or merely that there were so many pieces lying around the sites that they were easily transferred to later contexts.

Blown glass

Several forms that had been introduced after the middle of the first century BC continued to be developed and became more popular after about AD 70. Many of these occur only on sites in the western and north-western provinces and must have been made at glasshouses in the Rhineland or northern Gaul. One group of such vessels includes long-necked jugs with globular, discoid or conical bodies, often decorated with optic-blown ribbing (figure 20.8-10). They were very elegant, with long angular handles, sometimes with a moulded head medallion beneath, often identified as that of Bacchus or his guardian and companion, Silenus (figure 25). Sometimes this is replaced by a long pinched trail (figure 20.8, 10). Coloured varieties occur, in dark blue,

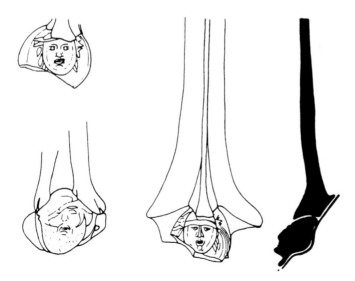

25. Glass masks from beneath the handles of jugs, found at various sites in Colchester, Essex. Scale ¹/₂.

wine, brown and amber glass, as well as blue-green, but never colourless. They were common on settlement sites and were also often included as grave-goods in burials, and a number of complete British finds have survived in this way. The group had evolved by about AD 60 and was most common from about AD 70-130. A few remained in use to the middle of the second century.

Closely related to these jugs was a form of globular ribbed jar with folded collar (figure 20.6). Again, they were common in later first- and early second-century contexts on settlement sites as well as in graves, they were made in coloured and blue-green glass, and body and base fragments are difficult to distinguish from those of the jugs. Similar also in style and colours were cylindrical ribbed bowls with folded rims (figure 13.13), which had been introduced around the middle of the first century AD, continued to be popular until the middle of the second century and were used until about AD 170.

Smaller jugs with spouted rims were also used at this time. Those of late first- and second-century date often had short necks and wide rims pinched in at the side to form the spout. A fine complete blue-green example with decorated mouth and handle was included in a burial at Colchester (figure 20.5).

Glass drinking cups from AD 70 were usually colourless and were decorated in a variety of ways. One of the earliest forms was the indented beaker, which appeared during the middle of the first century but was most common, in colourless, pale green and occasionally blue-green glass, from AD 70 to early in the second century (figure 19.12). Similar in shape, appearance and date was a type of beaker decorated with arcaded, pinched trails (figure 19.13).

Colourless drinking vessels decorated with facet-cutting were very popular from AD 65/70 to 130. Similarities can be seen between these vessels and the contemporary cast bowls and dishes described above (page 28) in that they were fashioned by grinding the external surface from a thick vessel blank. However, the shiny bloom on the inner surface shows that this group was produced by blowing. A variety of shapes and decorations was produced, but certain characteristics are shared by all. These include the truncated conical body, low foot-ring and high ridges below the rim and above the base, with a zone of cut decoration between. This decoration often consists of facets arranged in quincunx (figure 19.8), sometimes long, waving, jigsaw-like facets (figure 19.10), and rarely, as on a beaker from Caerleon, a figurative scene, in this case of a chariot race (figure 19.9). Occasionally cups and beakers with high-relief cut decoration were made. Many of the designs were similar to those produced during the same period by mould-blowing, with shells, ovals and rosettes (figure 19.11).

26. Glass cinerary urn buried in a cist of tiles, from Colchester, Essex. (Photograph by David Allen, reproduced with the permission of the Castle Museum, Colchester)

During the early and middle second century the commonest drinking cups were colourless carinated or cylindrical vessels decorated with bands of horizontal wheel-cut lines (figures 19.14-15).

Some large glass containers of the later first and second centuries have already been discussed above (pages 31-5), and others include large jars. Many survived more or less intact because of their use as cinerary urns in later first- and earlier second-century burials. Some were first made as domestic vessels and reused, but others may have been made expressly for this funerary purpose (figures 26-27).

Smaller unguent bottles and flasks were also made at this time. They were nearly always blue-green in colour and were made for convenience rather than beauty. The commonest unguent bottle form had a long cylindrical neck and a small conical or discoid reservoir for the contents. Occasionally a stamped trademark was impressed into the base when the glass was warm and pliable. This often takes the form of a name,

27. Glass cinerary urn buried in a lead box with a wooden lid inside a tomb under a barrow, Mersea Island, Essex. (Photograph by David Allen, reproduced with the permission of the Castle Museum, Colchester)

abbreviated or in full, such as CN.A.ING.A.V.M. on a vessel from Colchester or A.VOLVMNI IANVARI on one from Bolton Percy, North Yorkshire (figure 20.3). Sometimes the inscription incorporates the word PATRIMONI and is thought to refer to some form of imperial monopoly over trade in the perfumes contained in the bottles (figure 20.2 from a grave at Chester).

Also common at this time, as well as during the earlier third century, were small globular-bodied bath flasks. These had two small 'dolphin-shaped' handles by which they were suspended by a chain from the wrist; full of perfumed oil, they were carried in this way to the bath-house (figure 20.4). A few have been found with their metal handles intact.

5

Glass vessels AD 170–300

The glassware used in Britain and the other north-western provinces during the later second and third centuries consisted in the main of blown colourless or greenish vessels. Blue-green glass still appeared regularly, but there was hardly any coloured glass, no cast wares, and little or no mould-blown glass. The range of forms was far from limited, however, and various types of cut decoration continued to be popular, as well as trailing and tooling, and there was some use of optic-blowing and painting.

The popular drinking vessel during the earlier part of this period, from about AD 170 to 240, was a colourless cylindrical cup with fire-rounded rim and a double base-ring (figure 28.2). Occasionally it has a single trail beneath the rim (figure 28.1). Many examples occur on occupation sites of this date, and they were occasionally included in graves. They seem to have been the most numerous of any single variety of Roman glass cup, and several British sites have produced fragments of between fifty and one hundred vessels. From this huge output, two small groups were decorated, probably by enterprising artists working independently from the glass manufacturers. Both groups have characteristic design elements that indicate that each represents the work of one person or a small team.

The first group comprises cups with painted scenes usually inspired by the amphitheatre games, with wild beasts such as lions, leopards and bulls, often fighting each other or chasing stags. A few show gladiators, birds or swimming fish. Nearly all have a characteristic row of painted dots beneath the rim. Several complete vessels have come from graves found beyond the frontiers of the Empire in what is now eastern Germany and Denmark, and fragments have been found scattered throughout the north-western provinces, including Britain (figure 30). Nearly twenty small pieces have been found on sites all over Britain, with a particular concentration along Hadrian's Wall.

The other group of decorated cylindrical cups is known only from fragments, as no complete example has been found. These cups have hand-carved designs, often incorporating fish and palm fronds, together with letters from an inscription (figure 31). It has occasionally been suggested that the symbols on these vessels may have some Christian significance, but in view of their date, the fact that many have been found at military sites and the incompleteness of the evidence, this seems most unlikely. Perhaps as many as thirty to forty fragments have

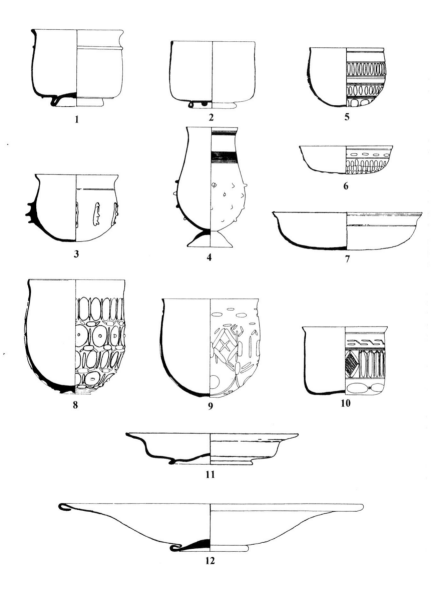

28. Some of the cups, bowls and plates that were popular during the period AD 170-270. Scale ¹/₄.

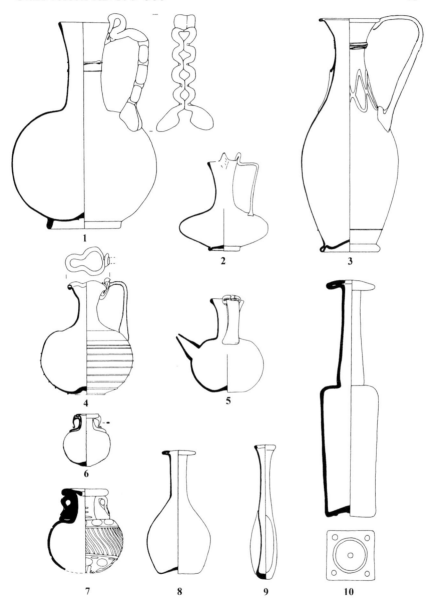

29. Some of the serving vessels and containers that were popular during the period AD 170-270. Scale ¹/₄.

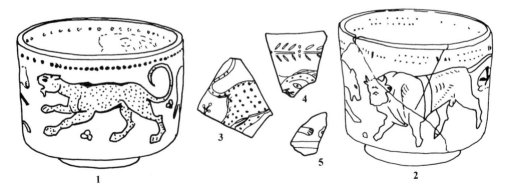

30. 1-2 Painted cups from graves in Denmark. 3-5 Fragments found in Britain: 3 Corbridge, Northumberland; 4 Chesters, Northumberland; 5 Housesteads, Northumberland. Scale ¹/₂.

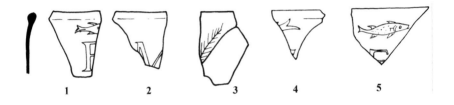

31. Engraved rim fragments from cylindrical cups: 1-2 Corbridge, Northumberland; 3 Woodburcote, near Towcester, Northamptonshire; 4 Verulamium, Hertfordshire; 5 Chesters, Northumberland. Scale ¹/₂.

now been found, of which about a quarter are from scattered sites in Britain.

Contemporary with these cups was a decorative group that encompasses an extremely wide and imaginative range of vessel shapes. They are called 'snake-thread glasses', because of the characteristic cross-hatched snake-like trails of opaque white, yellow and blue, or occasionally colourless, glass that were applied to the surfaces of the vessels, which were usually colourless. A rare variant has opaque white trails on a strongly coloured background. This is a decorative technique that was an integral part of the manufacture of the vessels, and there were production centres in both eastern and western areas of the Empire. Large numbers of complete vessels have been found as grave-goods in

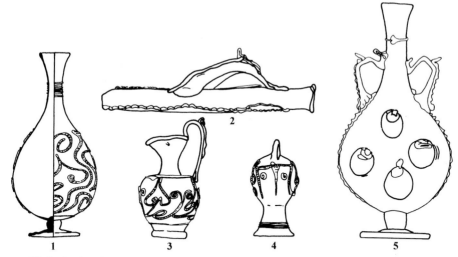

32. Snake-thread vessels from Cologne. Scale ¹/₄.

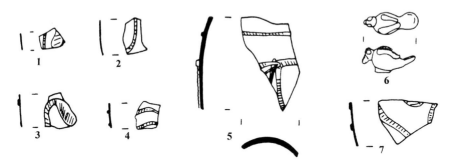

33. Snake-thread fragments from Britain: 1-5 Caerleon, Gwent; 6 York; 7 Verulamium, Hertfordshire. Scale ¹/₂.

burials in and around Cologne, and this has a strong claim to be a site of manufacture. Bowls, cups, stemmed beakers, jugs and flasks were decorated in this way, some of them imaginatively shaped like gladiators' helmets and sandals (figure 32.1-5). Unfortunately no complete snake-thread glasses have yet been found in Britain, although small fragments, easily recognised, occur quite regularly on domestic sites (figure 33.1-

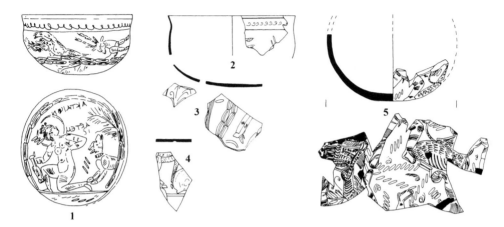

34. Vessels and fragments with figurative facet-cutting, with engraved details. Scale ¹/₄. 1 Bowl from a grave at Leuna-Merseburg, Cologne, depicting the myth of Actaeon and Artemis. 2-3 Fragments from Caerleon, Gwent, from similar vessels. 4 Fragment from Verulamium, Hertfordshire. 5 Fragments of a ?flask from Caerleon, Gwent.

7). One of the most elaborate shapes belonging to this general group, a flask with tiny birds perched in holes in the body (figure 32.5), may be represented by a bird figurine from York (figure 33.6).

From about AD 230 the cylindrical cups were replaced as the most popular drinking vessel by a hemispherical form, often decorated with pinched-out nipples and lugs (figure 28.3). These appear to have been much less numerous than their predecessors, but this may be because base and rim fragments are not so instantly recognisable. This form of decoration was used for other vessel shapes, too (figure 28.4), but had gone out of fashion by the end of the third century.

Cut and engraved decoration, introduced during the late first century, continued to be developed throughout the second and third centuries. Bowls that were shallow and curved, or deep and hemispherical, were the best shapes for showing such designs, and these were very popular. Sometimes the patterns of facets were abstract and geometric (figure 28.5-6), and sometimes figurative. Individual styles of cutting have been identified, particularly amongst glasses with figured scenes, which must represent the output of individual artists or schools. One such group consists largely of hemispherical bowls, with a characteristic curvilinear line beneath the rim, and a scene, usually from popular mythology, made from wheel-cut facets with hand-carved details. Several vessels have come from in and around Cologne, and this may be the origin of the group. One complete bowl depicting the myth of

Actaeon and Artemis, now in the British Museum, came from a third-century grave at Leuna Merseburg near Cologne (figure 34.1), and some of the fragments from British sites must come from similar vessels (figure 34.2-4).

Towards the end of the third century deep hemispherical or cylindrical bowls decorated with geometric patterns of facets combined with short cut lines became popular. Several complete or substantially complete British finds have survived (figure 28.8-9 from Verulamium, figure 28.10 from York).

Various glass jugs, both large and small, were being produced during the later second and third centuries. A small globular form with body spout was made at this time in glass, usually blue-green, as well as pottery, and is usually identified as a baby's feeding bottle, although this is by no means certain, and they may have been used to pour oil into pottery lamps (figure 29.5). Another small jug type, occurring in colourless as well as blue-green glass, has a globular or discoid body and short neck, with the rim pulled into a pointed spout either opposite or at right-angles to the handle (figure 29.2). Jugs with trefoil mouths, variously decorated, were also popular (figure 29.4).

Larger jugs with funnel mouths and globular bodies, often decorated with optic-blown ribs, were made during the third century. They occur in blue-green or colourless glass and often have a chain handle, formed from two strands of glass nipped together at intervals (cover photograph and figure 29.1). Some jugs with ovoid bodies also belong to the third century (figure 29.3).

Large glass containers are rare for much of this period, although some blue-green square bottles were still circulating during the early years, and some colourless cylindrical bottles and flasks were introduced before the end of the third century, to become more common during the fourth century (figure 35.1-2, 4). It is possible that containers made of some other material were replacing glass for a while, but even during the fourth century glass bottles were never as common as they had been during the late first and second centuries. There must have been some change in trading patterns, which could be difficult to identify from the archaeological record.

A form of globular-bodied flask with tapering neck was also introduced before the end of the third century (figure 35.3). These vessels were sometimes given elaborate cut decoration, and some large fragments from Caerleon, Gwent, with figurative facet-cutting have been identified as probably belonging to a vessel of this type (figure 34.5). The scene may show amphitheatre games or a story from mythology, and the style of cutting, with engraved details, is very similar to that on the Actaeon and Artemis bowls discussed above.

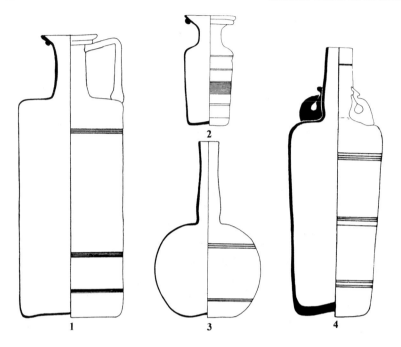

35. Some glass containers that were introduced during the second half of the third century AD and continued to be used into the fourth century. Scale ¹/₄.

A form of ovoid flask with concave base occasionally occurs at this time but is not easily identified in fragmentary form, so its popularity is hard to assess (figure 29.8).

Some smaller glass containers were widely used. Bath flasks continued to be common until the middle of the third century. Very many fragmentary blue-green examples and one better-quality colourless piece with cut decoration had been washed down the main drain of the legionary bath-house at Caerleon, Gwent, between AD 160 and 230 (figures 29.6-7, 36), and further bath-flask fragments were found at this site in contexts dating until the mid to late third century.

A few varieties of unguent bottle were circulating at this period. One, with indented body, made of colourless or greenish glass, occurs occasionally in burials but was not very common (figure 29.9). Another, with rectangular mould-blown body, is found quite frequently in late second- and third-century contexts in France, Belgium and elsewhere but is rare in Britain. It is known as the 'Mercury bottle' because of the

36. Colourless wheel-cut bath flask found in fragments in the drain of the legionary bath-house at Caerleon, Gwent. (Reproduced by permission of the National Museum of Wales)

moulded basal marking that often includes the figure of Mercury, god of commerce, with a purse, or sometimes animals that were particularly associated with him, such as a ram, a cock or a tortoise. Sometimes the basal marking includes letters; sometimes it comprises only a simple geometric design, as on a complete vessel from a grave at Chester (figure 29.10).

6
Glass vessels AD 300–410

A certain continuity of style can be seen in the glassware in use during the later third century and the earlier part of the fourth century AD. It was nearly all colourless or pale green, and decorative techniques included cutting and engraving, tooling, trailing, optic-blowing and some mould-blowing. Rims, particularly of bowls and cups, were usually finished by simply cracking them off and polishing them more or less smooth. As the century progressed, however, a decline becomes apparent in the range and quality of glassware produced. More and more yellow-green and pale olive-green glass was used, often with many tiny bubbles and other impurities visible within it. Elaborate cut decoration disappeared, and cruder decorations of applied coloured blobs, optic-blowing and some tooling and trailing were all that remained. The forces breaking up the Western Roman Empire were destroying the markets and trade routes of the glassmakers, as well as other manufacturers, and many of their skills were lost to northern Europe until the Renaissance period.

The common shapes for fourth-century drinking vessels were hemispherical cups and conical beakers. A variant of the former decorated with geometric facet-cutting, popular during the late third century, continued to be produced into the fourth, but they most often had simple horizontal wheel-incised lines (figure 37.1). Conical beakers were common throughout the period, in pale green and yellow-green glass, usually decorated with wheel-incised lines (figure 37.2-3). Shallow, curved segmental bowls were also a characteristic fourth-century form and were also probably used for drinking (figure 37.6-7). Popular decorative techniques included indenting, trailing or the application of simple geometric patterns of applied coloured blobs. A complete example of the last variety came from a grave of about AD 370 at Chignall Roman villa, Essex (figure 37.4). The slightly outflared, cracked-off rims of these vessels are usually the commonest recognisable glass finds on late Roman sites, such as villas.

More elaborate cutting and engraving techniques remained popular during the first half of the fourth century. These were usually employed to enhance drinking vessels of the forms described above, and several decorative styles have been identified. One close-knit group of vessels has free-hand engraving, showing either hunting, mythical or biblical scenes, often with an inscribed exhortation in Latin such as 'Good health to you and yours'. The style of the engraving is very characteristic,

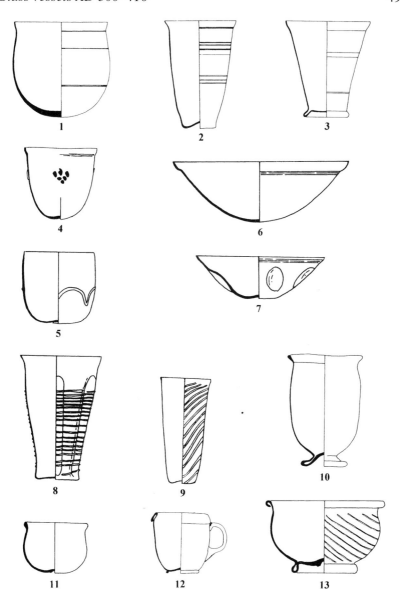

37. Some of the cup and bowl forms that were popular during the period AD 300–400+. Scale ¹/₄.

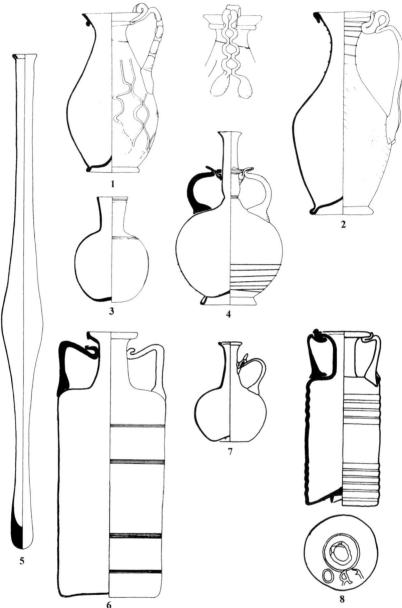

38. Some of the serving vessels and containers that were popular during the period AD 300–400+. Scale ¹/₄.

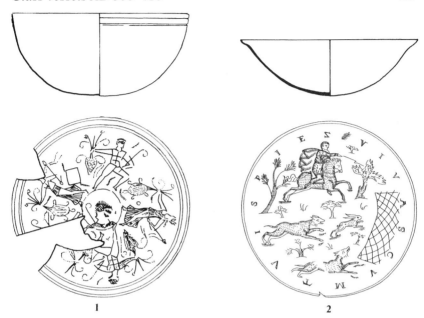

39. Bowls with cut and engraved figurative scenes: 1 Colliton Park, Dorchester, Dorset, Bacchic dancing scene; 2 Wint Hill, Somerset, hunting scene. Scale ¼.

with cross-hatched shading inside many of the outlines, and this too must represent the work of a single artist or group. Nearly fifty vessels and fragments are known, of which more than twenty, mostly fragments, have come from Britain. They are often described as the 'Wint Hill Group', after a fine complete shallow segmental bowl found at Wint Hill, near Banwell, Somerset, now on display at the Ashmolean Museum, Oxford (figure 39.2). Again, Cologne is seen as the probable manufacturing centre. A smaller group is characterised by figured scenes produced from fine short wheel-cut lines and patches of abrasion. One of the best-preserved British finds is a fragmentary bowl with a Bacchic dancing scene from Colliton Park, Dorchester, Dorset, on display in the Dorset County Museum in Dorchester (figure 39.1).

A further group of cups of the first half of the fourth century shows the technical ability of the glass-cutters to perfection. These were the cage-cups, or diatreta, so-called because almost the entire outer surface was cut and ground away, leaving an outer patterned network cage, which may be geometric or figurative, joined to the main body only by narrow bridges of glass (figure 40.1-3). Cologne has been suggested as one centre of production, and several cups have been found in graves there. Only a few very small but distinctive and recognisable fragments

have been found on British sites, at Silchester (Hampshire), Great
Staughton (Cambridgeshire) and Canterbury (Kent), but this is enough
to indicate that some of these valuable vessels were used in the province.

Serving vessels, presumably for wine, include ovoid jugs, which had
been introduced during the later third century but were much commoner
during the fourth. These have an outflared rim with self-coloured trail
beneath, often optic-blown ribbing, and either a ribbed or a chain handle.
Several substantially complete British finds have been preserved in late
Roman graves, including figure 38.1-2 from Colchester, Essex. A very
elegant form of two-handled flask may also have been used for serving
at the table, but some examples have such a narrow restriction between
neck and body that they would not have poured well and may have been
for show only. A very fine complete example has come from Colchester
(figure 38.4), and another, substantially complete, from a grave of AD
370-90 at Lankhills, Winchester, Hampshire (figure 41).

Several of the bottle and flask forms introduced during the second
half of the third century continued to be made during the fourth (figures
29.9, 35.1-4). Many of the cylindrical forms of the fourth century share
similar characteristics, and fragments are often difficult to assign to one
or the other. They were all made of colourless or pale green glass and
had cylindrical bodies decorated with horizontal wheel-incised lines,
short necks with flaring, fire-rounded rims and a self-coloured trail
beneath. Some were quite small, with no handles (figure 35.2), whilst
others were larger, with either one or two angular ribbed handles (figures
35.1, 38.6). Another cylindrical-bodied form, also with wheel-incised
lines, had a tapering neck and two 'dolphin' handles (figure 35.4).
These were presumably the late Roman counterparts of the common
blue-green bottles of the first and second centuries. Whilst they occur
quite regularly in graves in Britain, as elsewhere, and fragments are often

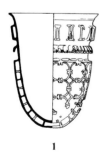   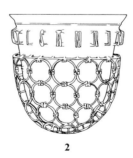   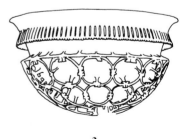

1   2   3

40. Diatreta: 1 Cologne; 2 near Novara, Italy; 3 ?Syria. A few small fragments from similar
vessels have been found in Britain. Scale ¹/₄.

41. Two-handled flask, green glass, from a grave of AD 370-90 at Lankhills, Winchester, Hampshire. (Copyright Winchester Excavations Committee)

found on domestic sites, they are never as dominant in late glass assemblages as blue-green bottle fragments were earlier and were presumably never as common. This may indicate a change in the quantity of the contents being traded or that some other material was being used for the rest of the containers.

Large 'pipette-shaped' unguent bottles, with long narrow body and central bulge, seem to occur only in late inhumation graves and perhaps had only a funerary use (figure 38.5 from Verulamium). Certainly the shape is not a very practical one for any domestic purpose.

One more late Roman bottle type is the mould-blown barrel-shaped bottle (figure 38.8). These sometimes had names moulded on the base, the most common being Frontinus, after whom the group is sometimes called. The distribution of these vessels suggests a manufacturing centre in northern France, and the overall form was very long-lived. Some,

42. One-handled barrel-jug, green glass, with the inscription FELIX FECIT on the base, from Faversham, Kent, late third century. (Copyright British Museum)

with only one handle, occur in second-century contexts, but most, including a variant with two handles, belong to the fourth century. A complete one-handled bottle made by Felix, possibly during the third century, was found at Faversham, Kent (figure 42), whilst a more recent find is a two-handled bottle with FRO on its base from a fourth-century grave at Butt Road, Colchester, Essex (figure 38.8).

Towards the very end of the Roman period colourless glass was entirely replaced by yellow-green or pale olive-green. Rims were folded or fire-rounded, and decoration was restricted to optic-blown ribs and trails.

These latest Roman vessels, from the second half of the fourth century and the beginning of the fifth, include ribbed tubular-rimmed bowls (figure 37.13), conical beakers and hemispherical bowls with fire-rounded rims (figures 37.9, 11), tall beakers with feet (figure 37.10), small cups with a single handle (figure 37.12), and small globular jugs with rod handles (figure 38.7). They represent the last Roman forms and mark the beginning of a series of Germanic or Anglo-Saxon glasses that differed in style and, eventually, chemical composition from what had gone before. Some, such as the Saxon claw beakers, showed considerable manufacturing skill, but the range and quantity of glassware circulating in north-western Europe was severely diminished. Glass no longer played such an important economic and social role in everyday life, and what Donald Harden, pioneer of glass studies, described as the Roman achievement – 'the ubiquity of glass in Roman times' – was lost.

7
Glass objects and windows

Glass was used not only for vessels during Roman times, but for a wide array of objects, full discussion of which lies beyond the scope of this book. Items of jewellery, such as beads and bangles, were common, as were small plano-convex discs, which could have been used as gaming pieces or for accounting. Glass tesserae were sometimes used in mosaics, usually to add lustrous detail when depicting water or eyes. Occasionally, whole mosaics were made of glass, although these tend to be set behind fountains rather than on the floor. Hairpins, cosmetic sticks, spoons and ladles were also made of glass.

Brief mention must be made here of windows, since these were often glazed in Roman times. The British climate must have provided a good incentive to fill window apertures with glass rather than open grilles, and most sites in the province produce some fragments of window glass.

The widespread production of window glass began during the first century AD, and the simplicity of the process suggests that most, if not all, would have been made locally. The window glass of the first three centuries AD is known by the term 'matt-glossy', because of its appearance. It was made by heating glass, probably reused fragments, to a temperature high enough to allow sluggish flow. It was then poured into some sort of tray, either wood, metal or stone, and tools were used to push it to the sides and into the corners. Its resulting appearance has a matt underside, often with impressions of wood grain or granular stone, and a glossy upper side, with a characteristic 'thumb' edge and often tool impressions at the corners (figure 43.2). It is usually blue-green in colour, occasionally colourless, and between 2 and 5 mm thick. Very few complete or reconstructable panes have been found, but one from a bath-house at Corbridge, Northumberland, was 600 mm square, and another, from Garden Hill, Sussex, was 270 by 230 mm. The size of some panes as manufactured was altered by grozing. Occasionally lime mortar and brick cement are found on or with glass fragments, and this must have acted as putty, setting the pane into the window recess (figure 43.1). The thickness and colour of the panes would result in the admission of daylight but would not afford a view in or out.

Another method of making window glass seems to have been introduced during the second century AD but was not widely adopted until after about AD 300. This involved blowing a large bulb of glass, which was elongated into a cylinder by swinging and manipulating the

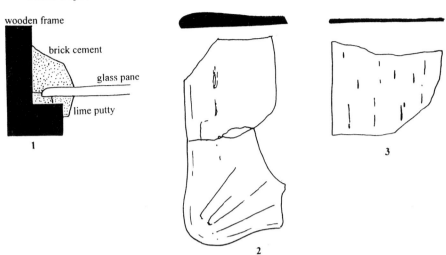

43. 1 Reconstructed window setting from Caerleon, Gwent (after Zienkiewicz). Scale ¹/₄. 2 'Thumb' edge fragment of cast matt-glossy window glass showing tool marks where soft glass was pushed to the corners of the tray. Scale ¹/₂. 3 Rounded edge fragment of cylinder-blown window glass, with elongated bubbles. Scale ¹/₂.

blowpipe. After removal from the pipe, the cylinder was cut whilst still warm, using a pair of shears, opened out and flattened into a pane of glass. This procedure results in 'double-glossy' panes, often with parallel elongated bubbles visible within the glass. It is thinner, between 1.5 and 3 mm, usually pale yellow-green or olive-green, and would have been a little more transparent than the cast panes, but not completely see-through (figure 43.3). This method of manufacture, known as the muff process, was still widely used for windows until the nineteenth century.

58

8
Glossary of manufacturing terms and decorative techniques

Base finish: the undersides of vessels could be finished by simply flattening the bulb of the body, or making it slightly concave, or pushing it into a pointed kick, while the glass was still warm and pliable. Alternatively a base-ring could be folded from the vessel wall, or it could be added as a separate trail of glass. Sometimes a foot, blown separately and cut to the required size, would be fused to the underside of the vessel.

Cameo glass: glass of one colour is covered, often by casing, with one or more layers of contrasting colours. The outer layers are then carved to produce a cameo design, as on gemstones.

Carving: glass is removed from the surface of a vessel or object using hand-held tools, such as files, points and gravers.

Casing: a preformed blank of glass is made, which then has a gob of hot glass of a contrasting colour inflated inside it. The two layers fuse and are then inflated together.

Cast glass: a general term given to vessels which have not been produced by blowing. The commonest techniques are described on page 7.

Cutting: decoration is produced by removing glass from the vessel surface by grinding with a rotating stone fed with an abrasive suspended in water. Popular designs included both geometric facets, sometimes combined with patterns of short cut lines, and figurative scenes. Simple horizontal wheel-cut lines and grooves occur very commonly, either separately or in bands.

Engraving: producing decoration on the vessel surface by holding it against a rotating copper wheel fed with an abrasive.

Fire-polishing: the reintroduction of the vessel into the furnace, either to smooth the vessel walls, or to finish the rim by rounding and thickening.

Flashing: the opposite of casing, achieved by dipping a gob of hot glass of one colour into a batch of molten glass of a contrasting colour before inflation.

Free-blown glass: vessels produced by inflation through a blowpipe, shaped by manipulation and tooling, without using any moulds.

Grozing: the removal of pieces of glass to make a fragment suitable for some secondary purpose. This can be achieved by using a grozing iron and snapping off the pieces, or by knapping, as with a piece of flint. Reuse of broken vessel pieces was common during the Roman period. Strong vessel bases, in particular, were often refashioned into small dishes or lids or circular gaming pieces.

Handles: these would be added at a late stage of the production process, after completion of the vessel body but before annealing. Usually a blob of glass was applied to the shoulder and drawn up, shaped and applied to the neck or beneath the rim. Handles occur in many shapes: flat, round, ribbed, sometimes with pinched decoration and/or a pinched tail adhering to the body. Occasionally they were fashioned from two strands pinched or twisted together to form 'chains' or 'ropes'.

Lathe-cutting: the vessel, or a shaped blank, is mounted and turned with the aid of a bow or handled wheel, whilst a tool fed with abrasive is held against the surface to polish it, or to modify the profile.

Marvering: the hot pliable glass is rolled over a polished flat surface in order to smooth out the vessel wall before or during blowing. Sometimes added trails or blobs of contrasting colours are marvered flush with the surface, to produce a marbled or mottled effect after blowing.

Millefiori glass: Italian for 'one thousand flowers', the term was coined by Venetian glass-workers to describe mosaic glass.

Mould-blown glass: vessels produced by blowing into a decorated mould, usually in two or three parts, made of fired clay, metal or stone.

Optic-blowing: the hot glass is first blown into a patterned mould, usually ribbed, then free-blown, so that the pattern expands and swirls with the shape of the body.

Painting: the addition of pigments as decoration to the outer surface of a cold finished glass vessel.

Rim finish: vessel rims could be finished by folding whilst the glass was still warm and pliable, or they could be reintroduced to the furnace and fire-rounded and thickened. Alternatively, the vessel could be left to cool, then scored and cracked off to form a rim at the desired position.

Rotary-polishing: smoothing the vessel surface when cold by holding it against a rotating wheel fed with an abrasive, such as emery.

Tooling: shaping hot pliable glass with tools such as tongs and pincers, to produce such decorations as indents, pinched-out nipples and pinched trails.

Trailing: strands of glass drawn out from a gather and applied to the surface of a vessel as decoration. They can be self-coloured or contrasting, left proud from the vessel surface or marvered into it. Spiral trails around part or all of the neck and/or body were quite common, and sinuous snake-thread trails were also popular for a time.

9
Further reading

Cool, H.E.M., and Price, Jennifer. *Roman Vessel Glass from Excavations in Colchester, 1971-85*. Colchester Archaeological Report 8, Colchester Archaeological Trust and English Heritage, 1995. Discussion of British glass is most often found in individual site reports, of which this is the most comprehensive and up-to-date.

Harden, D.B.; Hellenkemper, H.; Painter, K.; and Whitehouse, D. *Glass of the Caesars*. Olivetti, Milan, 1987. Glossy catalogue of an exhibition held at the British Museum, with excellent illustrations, and introductory chapters on techniques of manufacture.

Price, Jennifer, and Cottam, Sally. *Romano-British Glass Vessels: A Handbook*. Council for British Archaeology, 1998.

Strong, D., and Brown, D. *Roman Crafts*. Duckworth, London, 1976. Includes a chapter on glass by Jennifer Price.

Journals

Glass News, published by the Association for the History of Glass Ltd, keeps subscribers up-to-date on studies of historic glass.

Journal of Glass Studies, published annually by the Corning Museum of Glass (Corning Glass Center, Corning, New York 14830), includes articles on glass of all periods from all around the world.

10
Museums

Roman glass has been found in some quantity at all excavated sites of
the right date, and therefore all museum displays with a strong Roman
element will include vessel glass. The most outstanding collections in
Britain are listed here. Visitors are advised to find out the opening times
before making a special journey.

Ashmolean Museum of Art and Archaeology, Beaumont Street, Oxford
   OX1 2PH. Telephone: 01865 278000. Some British finds, including
   the Wint Hill bowl, and vessels from around the world.

British Museum, Great Russell Street, London WC1B 3DG.
   Telephone: 0171-636 1555. British finds, including a number of
   complete vessels, are displayed in the Roman Britain galleries,
   and there are famous vessels from around the world in the Greek
   and Roman departments.

Castle Museum, Castle Park, Colchester, Essex CO1 1TJ. Telephone:
   01206 282939.

Chesterholm Museum (The Vindolanda Trust), Bardon Mill, Hexham,
   Northumberland NE47 7JN. Telephone: 01434 344277.

Corbridge Roman Site Museum, Corbridge, Northumberland NE45 5NT.
   Telephone: 01434 632349.

Corinium Museum, Park Street, Cirencester, Gloucestershire GL7 2BX.
   Telephone: 01285 655611. Reconstruction of Roman glass window.

Grosvenor Museum, 27 Grosvenor Street, Chester, Cheshire CH1 2DD.
   Telephone: 01244 402008.

Museum of London, London Wall, London EC2Y 5HN. Telephone:
   0171-600 3699. More than thirty pieces of Roman glassware on show,
   many of them complete, as well as a display on Roman glass-working
   in the City of London.

Pilkington Glass Museum, St Helens, Lancashire. A new museum is being planned to open by 2000. Extensive displays will illustrate the evolution of glassmaking crafts and techniques from antiquity to the present day.

Roman Legionary Museum, High Street, Caerleon, Gwent NP6 1AE. Telephone: 01633 423134.

Royal Albert Memorial Museum, Queen Street, Exeter, Devon EX4 3RX. Telephone: 01392 365858.

Verulamium Museum, St Michaels, St Albans, Hertfordshire AL3 4SW. Telephone: 01727 819339.

Winchester City Museum, The Square, Winchester, Hampshire. Telephone: 01962 848269.

Yorkshire Museum, Museum Gardens, York YO1 7FR. Telephone: 01904 629745.

Index

Numbers in italic refer to pages with illustrations.